The Contemporary Condition book series offers a sustained inquiry into the contemporary condition from a range of perspectives by key commentators who investigate contemporaneity as a defining condition of our historical present. Contemporaneity refers to the temporal complexity that follows from the coming together in the same cultural space of heterogeneous clusters generated along different historical trajectories, across different scales, and in different localities. With the overall aim of questioning the formation of subjectivity in time and the concept of temporality in the world now, it is a basic assumption that art can operate as an advanced laboratory for investigating processes of meaning-making and for understanding wider developments within culture and society. The series identifies three broad lines of inquiry for investigation: the issue of temporality, the role of contemporary media and computational technologies, and how artistic practice makes epistemic claims.

AF207340

Sternberg Press

THE
CONTEMPORARY
CONDITION

THE CONTEMPORARY CONDITION 14

Co-existence of Times—A conversation with John Akomfrah
Johanne Løgstrup

Published by Sternberg Press, 2020

© 2020 John Akomfrah, Johanne Løgstrup, Sternberg Press,
Aarhus University, and ARoS Aarhus Art Museum

Series edited by Geoff Cox & Jacob Lund

Published in partnership with ARoS Aarhus Art Museum
and The Contemporary Condition research project
at Aarhus University, made possible by a grant
from the Danish Council for Independent Research,
September 2015—August 2018.

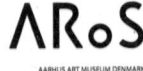 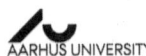

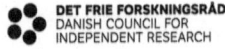

contemporaneity.au.dk

Design: Dexter Sinister
Printing and binding: BUD Potsdam
Paper: Vivus 89
Photo credits: Courtesy of Smoking Dogs Films
Transcription: Therese Henningsen
Proofreading: James Day
Thanks to Geoff Cox, Lotte Folke Kaarsholm, Anne Kølbæk Iversen,
David Lawson, Jacob Lund, and Ellen Otzen
Supported by Danish Arts Foundation

ISBN 978-3-95679-571-8

Sternberg Press
Caroline Schneider
Karl-Marx-Allee 78
D-10243 Berlin
www.sternberg-press.com

Distributed by The MIT Press, Art Data, and Les presses du réel

Co-existence of Times—A conversation with John Akomfrah

Johanne Løgstrup

INTRODUCTION

Conversations are provisional and unpredictable, but they have the potential to put us in contact with people from other places and times—or as John Akomfrah says, when confronted with conversation as a method of working, one can retrieve things.

This conversation originates from a special interest in the work of Akomfrah. Since the early 1980s as part of the collectives Black Audio Film Collective and Smoking Dogs FIlms, respectively, he has worked with film montage, and over the years, turned these into rich, multilayered video installations. In his works he brings poetic, ethical, and political questions into play by investigating topics such as collective memory, diaspora, and identity in a contemplative way. With this conversation I wanted to understand in more depth how Akomfrah deals with the understanding of time in his work: time as a concrete aspect of film media and montage, and how art articulates temporality, but also how art can be a useful approach to rework an understanding of historical time into the present. The technique of montage forces sequences of images into the same time and space by placing film clips from various sources next to each other. This allows the viewer to experience connections across time and space in her/his/their present. Akomfrah's works can be seen to articulate the contemporary condition in sensuous ways, making contemporaneity—or contemporaneities—something that can be directly experienced.

In the conversation we begin by talking about the methodology of his video works and how montage deals with temporality. He defines montage not only as a technique but as an ethic, an ontology in which differences are brought together. Further on we go into more detail about his process of editing and he describes the way he uses montage as a method of persuasion where each film clip is placed in connection with another. This allows for a non-hierarchical ordering and establishes a dialogue between film clips. We then discuss about the notion of diaspora and how to give voice to untold histories. Akomfrah uses the phrase "the enigma of arrival" and describes how this depicts the position of the migrant as someone who is always marked by her or his arrival. We also talk about how several of his seminal works came into being in what is now history. In this connection he explains how the *doppelgänger* can be used as a motif to describe the feeling among the young black population in the 1970s and '80s in Britain—a motif that still resonates today when we deal with identity questions and which reminds us how this is still a necessary concern that we need to keep on discussing. We should continue to have conversations across time in order to relate to a heterogeneous history and to evocate differences and similarities in our present.

The conversation took place in the Smoking Dogs Films studio in Hackney, London, October 2018.

THE MONTAGE: FROM TECHNIQUE TO ETHIC

Johanne Løgstrup: From the beginning of your career, you have worked with montage. Where did that interest in montage come from?

John Akomfrah: Prosaically, one would have to say it started from an interest in Russian cinema and Russian aesthetics, especially the writings of Sergei Eisenstein and Lev Kuleshov. The realization that I understood what it meant in cinema suddenly did something extraordinary, because I started to see that gesture in operation in other art forms. So, you look at Trees at l'Estaque *by Georges Braque from 1908, and you see the same strategy at work. It's like taking a slice of this and then juxtaposing it in order to establish a relation to that. The first time you read any of the modernists, you think, okay, this is the same thing.*

What that recognition of montage in cinema did was alert me to the possibility for this method of approaching temporality, which was certainly not unique to the cinema and it wasn't unique to "editing." Initially, it felt like an approach rather than a technique. As I grew older, I realized that it's actually an ethic. It slowly dawned on me that this was about the way in which one accepted the coexistence of difference. One accepted the idea that things, which are seemingly mutually exclusive from different worlds, things with different ontologies almost, can be brought into a relationship. No more than that, just a relationship to each other. This is really what montage said convincingly. Somehow in that encounter other possibilities could emerge, which were not wholly reducible to any of these parts. This relationship is creating a kind of spectacle or excitement or insight or profundity, which was not a result of component A or B or C or D for that matter.

Separately, none of them could have come to this way of seeing, but it was somehow the very act of forcing them into this collision that this other state, this other ontology almost emerges. Apart from anything else, even when I lost faith in it as a cinematic tool or device, I kept hold of that ethic, that philosophical understanding of what it was trying to get at. And I still believe that.

JL: Tell me about that period where you lost belief in it, how did that come about?

JA: A number of people were trying to understand the same thing, very recently. It became conveniently called the "death of cinema," because we're all trying to mark the passage of time. There was a major recognition. Something had felt superseded by a new phenomenon, whether this was about trying to understand a passage from the French new wave to Transformers or European art cinema to people like Bill Viola, you just sensed that something had complicated the relationship between your understanding of what constitutes the moving image and how it was currently manifesting itself.

I worked in cinema and I became disenchanted with it, not so much as a mode of working, but as an industry. I understand now very clearly that it's not so much that something died, but that different things came into being at the same time, so in a sense we accepted that there was one regime of truth, which was what narrative cinema wants. That narrative cinema would have as its high point the Hollywood system on the one hand or Indian cinema on the other, and as its counterpoint European art cinema. That sense of the world neatly arranged into geographies of cinemas is what has disappeared. Not because Hollywood films stopped being made or that no more films were being made in Indian cinema, but in the interstices between these geographies new continents started to emerge.

They didn't just emerge to contribute to just that old model of what cinema is, even though everybody wanted, that to be the case. So, the first time you see Apitchatpong Weerasethakul's Uncle Boonmee, for instance, that it wasn't just cinema as you knew it, there was something genuinely different. So different, in fact, that the idea that it and a Martin Scorsese film existed in the same world seemed just too big a leap to make. So, you can say that there are different national cinemas, but that didn't seem enough to understand these formations. It's not just the fact that Weerasethakul came from that part of the world, that he was Thai. That in itself didn't seem enough to describe these differences. At that point my belief in the cinema as a kind of unified entity took a bit of a knock.

It became a matter of honor, and a matter of survival, frankly, that you started to think through other possibilities for yourself. I wanted a space of authorship that didn't seem overly prescribed. I wanted something that was slightly less driven by forces outside of itself, and increasingly the gallery world seemed that space, because frankly if you wanted to starve, if you wanted to have the freedom of starving no one seemed to care [laughing].

Once you get into it you realize that there's actually a bit more to it than that, but the initial euphoria of the early part of the 2000s was: "We have this new space and we don't have to listen to anyone, no one is telling us that this is the best way to make a film." More importantly, it seemed as if you were walking into a space where you could genuinely make a difference. Since time-based work wasn't really the engine of the art world, no one was really paying that much attention. It didn't really matter that it's not painting or sculpture or anything. It felt as if part of the freedom was to begin to put into place what could be the rules by which this time-based space is measured. That was attractive. Most of the time in your life you're chasing what people are telling you. So, to suddenly be in this space where you could say: "We're making the rules." That felt incredibly liberating.

JL: Along that line, most artists and art historians who work with the montage either use space or time. Aby Warburg worked with montage in space and, as you mentioned, Eisenstein and many other filmmakers of course worked with montage in time. Can we go further into what kind of techniques these are and why you approached both?

JA: There was always something slightly strange. The conventional wisdom in cinema was that two of the key exponents of different kinds of montage came from different worlds. If you take Eisenstein and Andrei Tarkovsky, they are supposed to be almost polar opposites, in fact Tarkovsky talked about Eisenstein as if he were the devil [laughing]. He brought this diabolic system of shortening time and how dare he. Actually, it's not wholly accurate, that way of seeing montage. If you take Tarkovsky's Mirror, violent ruptures of time are not what is being foregrounded. The longue durée of it is in fact exactly that. The real feel of Mirror is precisely that even though it feels like it's about space, it's really about the experience of time. The move from color to black and white, from his childhood to Moscow, his mother's life, war, all of it is in a way this kind of search for a moment in time, which could be fixed as the moment of real insight. It can't, so it keeps shuffling between these different modes looking for this vantage point.

   The same with Eisenstein, his films are really about trying to take you into a kind of moment in the Russian past, which isn't just a time, it's also a space. So, the orchestration of movement, of time, for instance in the famous "Odessa Steps" sequence from Eisenstein's Battleship Potemkin: Everybody says that's montage, but actually the thing that you're left feeling most strongly is this heightened, temporal sense of understanding of that place. Like he extends time. There are, in fact only 180 steps but in reality, as Chris Marker reminded us watching that sequence, you feel like they're three thousand! And the overwhelming sense isn't just of this stretch of time, but it's also of that place. The conventional dichotomy, therefore, between time and space is not entirely true.

The manipulation of temporality can be ordered to service something else too, which is the coexistence of different renditions of time itself. In Vertigo Sea there are a lot of clocks. Which merely asserts the fact that there isn't one time. It at least alludes to this idea that all three screens are happening simultaneously, in different times and different spaces. So that's all I mean by the orchestration of time as a kind of coexistence.

THE METHOD OF PERSUASION, THE PROCESS OF EDITING

JL: It's as if the cutting and editing are the real drivers in your work. What does cutting and editing mean to you in the creation of your works?

JA: The cutting and the editing is metaphorically my voice, but that voice is not for the viewer, it's for the other beings that I'm speaking to in the projects. All of these projects have multiple ontologies, multiple beings at the center of them, all of whom say they are unique. Everything, in order to exist, has to assert its uniqueness, which makes it very difficult to arrive at a commonwealth, to get different things to sit together. The montage is a kind of method of persuasion. The editing is a method of persuading different slices from different projects, some I originated, some somebody else has shot, others I bought, to sit together. It's about saying to all

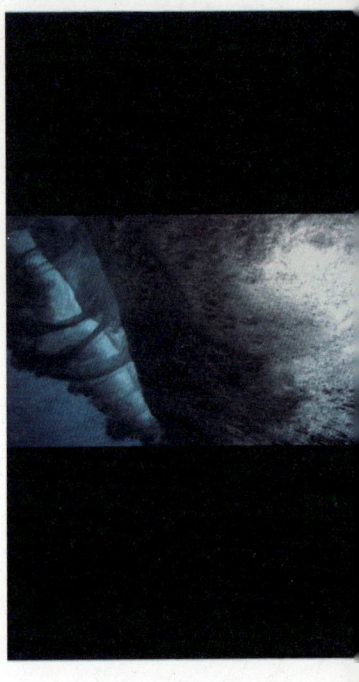

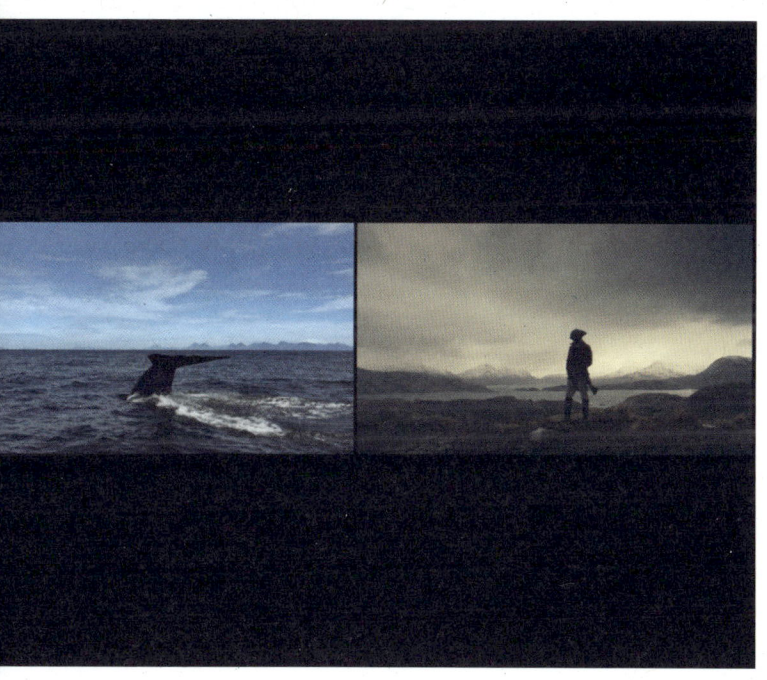

Vertigo Sea (2015) is a meditation on the aquatic sublime, where it brings together a collection of oblique tales and histories that speak to the multiple significances of the ocean and mankind's often troubling relationship with it. Touching upon migration, the history of slavery and colonization, war, and conflict and current ecological concerns, it is a narrative of man and nature, of beauty, violence, and of the precariousness of life. *Vertigo Sea* draws upon the books Herman Melville's *Moby-Dick* (1851) and Heathcote Williams's epic poem *Whale Nation* (1988), a harrowing and inspiring work that charts the history, intelligence and majesty of the largest mammal on earth.

of them, all these discrete fragments: I don't want you to lose your identity, that's not what we're trying to do here, so you don't have to become a scene in the conventional narrative sense, but I want a dialogue. I want you to talk to each other. Because if you can do this impossible thing, then there's hope for all of us. Dichotomies are in the project itself, in the material.

Vertigo Sea *has a lot of material from the BBC archive, from the Natural History Unit and the News and Current Affairs departments. I'm not trying to say that all of these divisions don't matter. They will continue to exist after I'm done, but for the purpose of this project they need to come to this proverbial Arthurian Round Table[1] and agree to a form of sociality, which is tentative, provisional, and open-ended. Basically, if everything in a piece just refuses to talk to each other, then that's the result. So, it's a kind of plea on my part. It's a sort of a gentle nudge to the footage, saying:* "Just sit there for five seconds, if you can." *And the really important thing is this: everything that you finally see, that I also get to see finally, is the result of all the people who've said yes, all the fragments that said yes. But the job is to decide when something is saying no, because they say that a lot. They say:* "You know what, I don't think this is going to work. I really don't like that dolphin we just can't speak." *So, the editing hand is as much about licensing that coexistence as terminating it. You have to put things together and then go, okay — sometimes, basically it's about taking things out, it's not always about putting things in.*

At that precise moment in the edit, when that seal is there in the sky, we need to leave, because immediately after that he would turn that way or that way and he would say: "Are you guys still here?" *[laughing]. There's the method of having to arrive at a language between yourself and the*

1. The Round Table referred to is King Arthur's famed table in the Arthurian legend, around which he and his knights congregate. As its name suggests, it has no head, implying that everyone who sits there has equal status.

material, which allows them to concede, to be at your service for a duration. And deciding when that duration has been met or fulfilled is what the editing is about as well as the conversation with the material.

It's like a private language that you have to formulate, a kind of Esperanto that will not be spoken after this project, because none of these things give you permanent license. Everyone of them is provisional, they'll say: "Okay, I'll do this and then I'm off." I noticed it feels like a banalization of a process. It feels like a conversation, in which you have to really accept that things you shot have ontologies. They don't do just what you want, just because you shot something, because all you did effectively was capture a fragment of time, in a particular way, in a space. So, I can go to Greenland, as I did. We shot quite a lot of stuff, some of which metaphorically just said: "No. I just don't like those guys, I don't want to be in the same room with them." But I have to accept that this is not a statement of hate, a statement of arrogance or even a statement of narcissism, even though sometimes it's all of those things. If I accept the possibility that it's not those things, then I can at least try to see what it is they see. Why is this sequence not sitting well?

In Purple, we shot two sequences on two different parts of Greenland. One was a man on a dog sleigh. The other was with a man walking to a hydroelectric plant. To make the sequence all I wanted to do was to have a journey and then an arrival, and I just couldn't get it to work. Every time I put the two sequences together, three screens of a dog sleigh cutting through ice and then we arrive at the hydroelectric plant, we cut to that, a man walks in, and it just didn't work. It slowly dawned on me, little things, like the light and the quality of ice, just didn't agree. You could see that the ice in the hydroelectric plant was old and slightly more crystallized, whereas the dog sleigh sequence in the snow was slightly softer, so even the ice refused to talk to

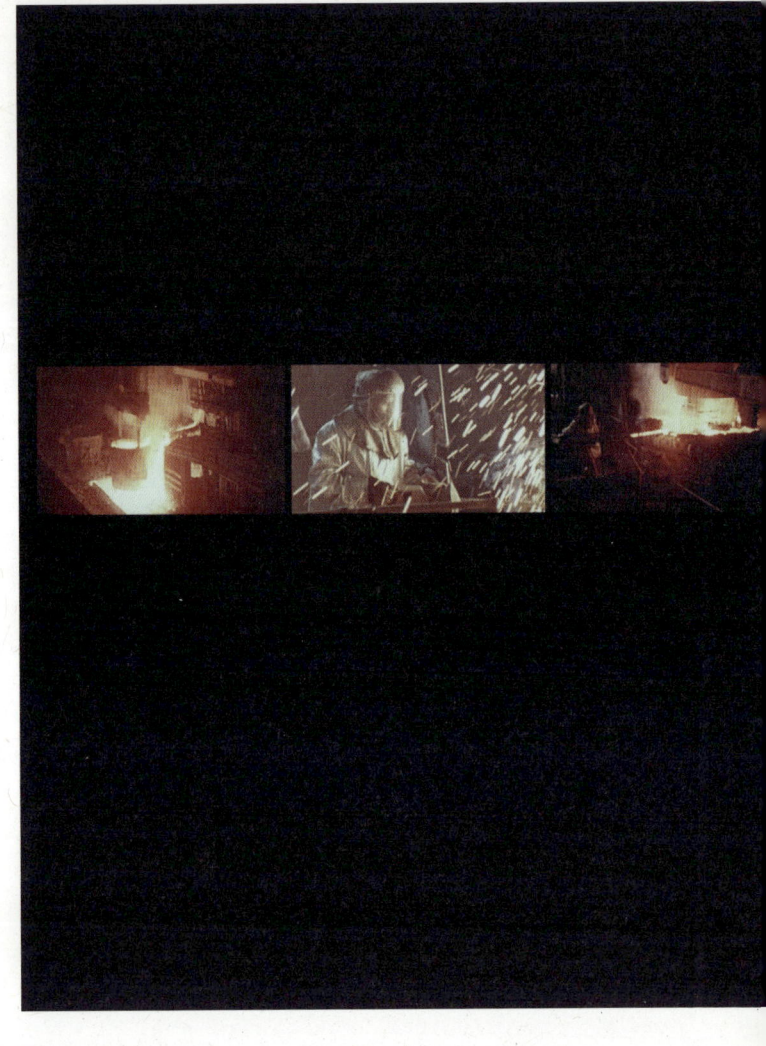

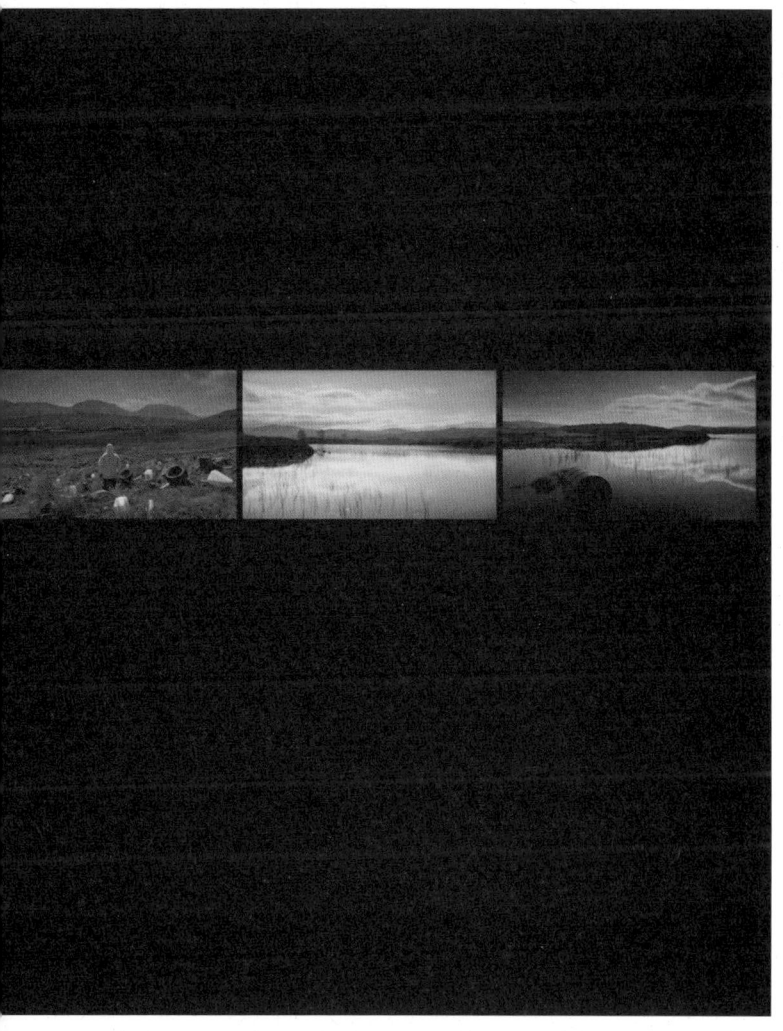

Purple (2017) focuses on the vitality and volatility of the natural world, where it concentrates on the human impact on the environment and the (be)coming of the Anthropocene. Weaving together a number of ecological and philosophical conversations—shifting weather patterns, the memory of ice, plastic oceans, rising sea levels, extreme weather events, biotechnology and AI—the work brings together a collage of ideas, images and sounds. *Purple* draws on a vast array of archival and electroacoustic source material as well as newly shot material.

each other [laughing]. I could have decided at that moment to not listen to either. I could have gone that route, but I didn't because in that particular instance I needed a much more harmonious sense of passage of time. I needed it to be more like, an hour ago a man was riding through the snow and then he arrives an hour later at this point. They wouldn't say that. If I needed it to say three days later, maybe they could have, or a week later maybe, but not an hour. So, what the two scenes were gently trying to tell me was that this cannot be seamless, and if you need the seamlessness, one of us has to go. So occasionally when images say things, it's not always hostile, you just need to understand, firstly what is the priority — am I trying to come up with something which feels like a contestation of time and space or something slightly more harmonious? The answer is usually what you need to arrive at in order to decide whether they sit together or not.

I've learned to trust two things simultaneously. One is my sense of propriety, but the other is also the implicit sense of decorum that all images and all material have. I have to trust both. I can't just assume that this is just inert material which does what I want. I enter into the projects trying to tease out from the material something that feels as if it's a middle way for both myself and the material. I force it if I think it's necessary for this conflict to be made apparent to everybody else, but if I don't need the conflict then I let it go away.

JL: In your work, so many connections across space and time are brought together, for instance in Vertigo Sea, you bring whale fishing together with the transatlantic slave trade and today's migration crisis. So, I would be interested to hear your thoughts on the disconnects and the connects.

JA: My aim is not to create just this melange where nothing has any authenticity or uniqueness. For instance, I don't think

I'm saying that the killing of humpback whales in the North Atlantic Ocean has either the same weight, value, political narrative or otherwise as the drowning at sea of Africans at the height of the trade. What I am saying though is that there are overlaps and there are almost certainly proximities, affective or emotional, intellectual or otherwise, which you can only maintain, which don't exist if you have a "hierarchy," which I don't. This hierarchy can only be maintained if you think the humpback whale is just an "animal" with no feeling, no brains, which I don't believe. I'm not saying the humpback whale is a human being, but I'm also not saying it's a mere "animal." To have a project in which the two species with different ontologies or different experiences of being, different ways in which being is manifested in their existence, does not then mean that they're the same. In other words, to register and recognize the existence of something called ontology, you have to also register that it might just be spread across a variety of species, things, and I happen to do that.

I don't feel it's a reductionist project. I want someone who is merely interested in the whale trade, who thinks that's the most important thing, to also just momentarily consider that the technologies that allowed whaling to happen were also the same technologies that allowed the transatlantic slave trade to flourish. We need to consider the natural coexistence of things and to just look at things in a slightly different way. For instance, we have a system of mourning as human beings, saddened by the passage of something, a life for instance. And the way we express that is to cry. So, if you wanted to find different ways of registering the melancholic beyond the human, how does that happen? How could you do that? If you don't want to say, "Oh, the birds are flying in a sad way" [laughing], then there has to be a way in which one can orchestrate affective states. That things and species just get to embody, don't have to feel it or do it, but just embody it. The value of montage is to see the death of a humpback whale immediately before the spring awakening of butterflies in New Mexico. Can they coexist in a way that creates a system of mourning? Yes, I think so. Can it alert a viewer to the possibility that whales have spirit? Yes, why not? I'm happy to go along with that. Is that quasi-religious? Possibly. Do I care? No, not really. Because I don't think that the things that we throw at each other that are not innocent, necessarily need to blind us to the possibility, that they may well be true. That's only a problem if you think that the mystical is a problem, and I don't think the mystical is a problem.

THE ENIGMA OF ARRIVAL

JL: That leads me to ask about history, or rather the untold history, because it's like your working method and your relationship with history go hand in hand, as we've also touched upon. So, your technique is to give the past, present, and future new meanings?

JA: The question of the untold is obviously an important one, because in a way it so much describes what constitutes a diaspora. Diasporas are always characterized by various forms of absence, whether of institutions or monuments. Diasporas are always precariously perched on the precipice of oblivion. Sometimes the oblivion in question is cataclysmic, like the Holocaust, or merely the indifference of time. So, you could live in London and not know that in the eighteenth century there was a community of black Londoners in central London, which was as big as the community is now.

Proportionally speaking that's just the cruelty, indifference and malevolence of time to diasporas. Time knows that diasporas are not fortified by the institutions that give shape and structure to nations. And so, it wreaks vengeance on diasporas, all the time with this cruel insight.

That means if you either invest in excavating narratives, histories with either a small or a capital H, then this question of the untold is a major sentence or a major feature in your sentence. Why has this happened? The questioning of the untold remains this beguiling absence in all of this.

I'm interested in the untold. V. S. Naipaul is a writer I don't like very much, but he had one phrase from a novel that I really liked, The Enigma of Arrival. I thought that was a great phrase, a great way of describing the complexity of diaspora, the ways in which the enigmatic always marks your arrival. I'm interested in enigmas of arrival, because invariably just when you think something looks as if it's settled, it's either about to disappear or crop up somewhere else. It's just those enigmatic ways in which what appears to be simply a feature of diasporic lives actually marks quite a lot of other things too. So, we go a lot to Scotland, to the Highlands, Skye in particular, to film. One of the things you'll see in the Isle of Skye is just how beautiful it is. Part of what's striking about it is its desolateness, but that desolateness is not natural. It's one of the enigmatic features of the space, because it's only like that because people were forcibly removed in the Enclosure Acts of the 1700s. The English Crown forcibly removed people from those spaces in order to turn them into large farms.

JL: But how do we find the untold stories when there are no signs left?

JA: That's why some of the projects also become what they are. I try to make things that leave living rooms, vacant rooms in them for the unseen ghosts to have a place of refuge. Whatever Vertigo Sea is about, it's made with film material shot in places that have had all sorts of things that have happened to them. I can't know. I don't know. But if the work itself appears permeable, porous enough then it can be a place of refuge for the phantom. It's the other problem with this idea that unless a work is strident and appears to have a clearly defined voice, then it's somehow lacking something. What's more and more important for me is that there are windows, metaphorically speaking, windows and back doors and barn doors left open for other phantoms, other than those I'm trying to consciously conjure or hail into being, to also come in. It is perfectly fine for that to happen, so the untold need not be a resolution. It could remain a kind of enigmatic feature that just spectralizes, haunts the piece itself. For instance, when you look out to the sea in Vertigo Sea: How many beings have died there? I don't mean just people—but these abominable cruelties to other species. I think it's important that as you look at that sea you don't just think, that's just the space where that humpback whale died.

WORKS AND TIMES

JL: You have been working with themes such as diaspora, migration, and colonialism that have lately not only been present for people who have felt it on their own bodies, but now seem to be something that we all cannot ignore anymore. I think art can have an important way of making those of us who did not experience it on our own body understand some of these difficult issues that run through our society, and these are of course central themes through the whole of your work. I want to do a memory game with you. I would like you to go back to 1981, which was the year the riots in Brixton, London, and in Toxteth, Liverpool, happened. I would like you to describe the climate for black people in Britain at that time, if that's possible.

JA: If you understood the 1970s and '80s as the period of the doppelgänger, it'll make more sense. I think most young *people of color were aware that they had this life, which is the one they were present in: it was their life, their house, their mother, and that life was characterized by a set of norms, things you recognized and knew, things you liked and obviously disliked. You disliked when you were told to go to bed, you disliked not having as much food as your elder brother, and so on. They were kind of an attempt of conviviality. That conviviality was either your family life or your communal life. At the same time, you're also aware that there was this other space in which something or somebody, who looked really quite strikingly like you, also sat. That space was the space of the fugitive, the trespass, the crime, the fear, the anxiety. All of which seemed to center around this figure who felt like it was you but you didn't think that it was you. And then suddenly the two worlds come together and for any young person of color, this is the coming of race, the moments when you have this almost Lacanian mirror moment, when you encounter the* doppelgänger *and it becomes uncomfortably clear to you that in fact this mythos, this mythical figure is meant to be you: this is who the world you live in thinks you are!*

Most of us try to reject this double; I don't think anyone actually ever accepted that it was them. So, occasionally they would do things, either individually or collectively, to say that that's not them and that's what the Brixton riots felt like. To persuade a whole bunch of young people, who have really no necessary connection between each other, to all go into the street to throw stones, and burn cars, buildings, and so on. Something was holding this together; something has given shape to this. It's obviously their anger, it's obviously their hate, but the question is why? How can you get thousands and thousands of young people to gather together. You could either believe that they're doing this because there's something innately troubling about them, something biological almost that they share in an unspoken way, even with themselves. But there is a less "mythological" and more "phenomenological" way of looking at that moment: that those thousands of young people are taking this moment as a chance to exorcise, to literally get rid of the doppelgänger.

There was a special paramilitary unit operating in Brixton called the Special Patrol Group. That group implemented a very old law from 1824 called the Vagrancy Act, which was about loitering with intent. The way the loitering and the intent was defined was in terms of numbers, so if there was more than one of you standing on a street corner you could be seen to be loitering with intent. What the intent was didn't even have to be specified. So, young black kids, mainly male, were routinely being picked up using this 1824 law. Not every kid of color was picked up by this, but it was so routine that even the people who hadn't been picked up had heard of it, which is even more important: everybody had heard of this and this was a "potential condition of incarceration" for them. It gets to a point where you think — and I think that's the point of most of these riots — okay, there really ought to be something which tells me not to do this. Something that says this is really bad, it's wrong, the consequences will not be satisfactory. There should be something, but there isn't. Because when you pick up that stone and you're about to throw it, you can't think of any reason why throwing it is not a good idea. That's the frightening situation that most kids of color existed in. That they felt so outside of that society that it didn't matter whether they burned down a building or not. Of course, it mattered to the state but not to them.

Why would that happen? And here lies the importance of the doppelgänger: the indifference that the damage the stone could cause, could only happen if they, the rioters, sensed that at some point they had been placed somewhere else, which is a paradox and nobody understood it. Actually, there's a lot of talk about young black people, but it wasn't *anything that they recognized as them. You turn on the television: "Oh yes, and there was trouble and the young black kid was arrested." There was no absence of talk about who we were, but increasingly it felt like it was a conversation about another species, another being. You knew it couldn't have been an alien one, because the person who said it was you said it with utmost certainty. Sometimes, you would hear that same certainty in a voice saying that young black people of course, they have no idea who they are, because they're very confused about their culture and you think, really? I didn't think I was confused at all, but no one had asked me. This is going to sound weird, but it is true that this moment that appeared then and now as a moment of rupture was also a representational moment.*

It was almost like: okay, this is when we write ourselves into the narrative. You said, "I'm a troublemaker, but actually this is when I'm a troublemaker. Not when that guy, the police officer, was picking up and beating us up, this is what we are when we're trouble. Oh, and by the way: I actually did think about trying to say something constructive, but I couldn't think of anything constructive to say so I'm going to say this, which is not constructive at all, but that's what I want to say." So, there comes this weird moment of writing oneself into a space of sociality, which is completely antisocial, no question about it. No one is saying, "Oh this is right." They were doing it because they knew it wasn't right. That was the basis of doing it. They are saying: "This is the scale of my indifference to whether you think I'm good or not. This is the scale of how far I've gone. This is how far I don't care what you think, because clearly you haven't displayed any understanding of who I am, so I don't see why I need to do anything."

JL: Were you aware of this thinking back when you were doing Handsworth Songs?

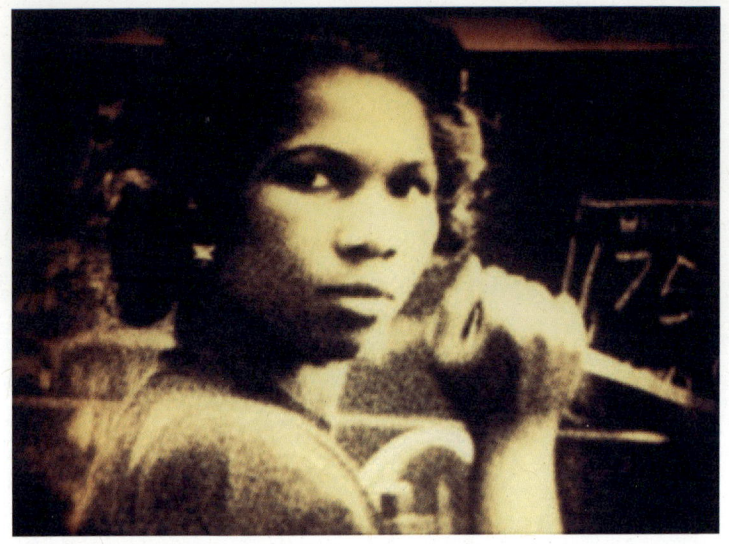

Handsworth Songs (1986) takes as its point of departure the civil disturbances of September and October 1985 in the district of Handsworth in Birmingham and in the urban centers of London. Running throughout the film is the idea that the riots were the outcome of a protracted suppression of black presence by British society. The film portrays civil disorder as an opening onto a secret history of dissatisfaction that is connected to the national drama of industrial decline. The "songs" of the title do not reference musicality but instead invoke the idea of documentary as a poetic montage tradition.

JA: Yes.

JL: So already then you knew that there needed to be some images of this situation?

JA: In my case it was very graphic. I was standing outside a train station in Brixton in '81, and I had this weird moment where you see the regime of truth deconstructed. You knew that there was a kind of conspiracy to define, because that's what it felt like. You didn't see where the stories were emanating from, so you just assumed it was a conspiracy. For me, Brixton was when I understood truth as a regime, because I saw it being constructed in front of me. You saw a group of police officers. They were banging on their shields with their truncheons and they were all really afraid, so they were going "kill, kill, kill." The next day there was a newspaper headline that said "Young Black Youth Chanting 'Kill, Kill, Kill.'" And that was when I saw what I would call the "enunciative and rhetorical regimes of race" at work. It just felt to the newspaper editorial regime that somehow this must be something that the black youth said, even if it was being said by the police. In fact, I understood then why it was necessary that it should be them who said it, because otherwise the whole thing didn't make sense. If these were marauding troublemakers just causing trouble, out to make mischief and malice, then of course they would say "kill, kill, kill." But no police officers, arbiters of civility, who were merely trying to arrest rioters would descend into anarchy. Could they?

Now, I'm not saying that the police officers in question wanted to kill anyone. They were just shouting because it was that moment of panic and fear and desperation, because they were all very young themselves. There's another possibility, which is that nobody was saying "kill, kill, kill," that those of us who thought we heard "kill, kill, kill" simply heard "heal,

heal, heal" or something else, that's also possible. The fact was that when it mutated into kill, when heal mutated into kill, it was definitely important for it to come from the mouths of young black kids not the police officers.

This is what differentiated somebody like me from a radical white filmmaker who would have felt the need to say something that empowers the young people of color, because they are there to understand why things are what they are: They would have to understand, they would have needed to avoid saying certain things that they thought would have been disempowering. I don't have that, because we needed to try understand something that didn't make sense. For instance, I never thought in '81 or '85 that everybody who turned up on the street had a motive and that they had worked it out in advance before they got there. If you spoke to them two weeks later, probably they would have said, "Yes, there was a motive." I'm not sure that that's how subjectivity works. I'm certainly not sure that that's what transpired.

The more likely unfolding scenario was something like: People heard that something was happening, then went into the streets and were empowered by the presence of others who were either friends or people who they felt understood them. For probably the majority of the people in the street, and this is a really sad thing, it's the first time they would have felt like they belonged to a country, because there was more than their family and a football team on the street. All of them were of the same opinion. It was a kind of perverse way of coming into sociality. A perverse way in which people discovered each other, saying, "Oh we got power, oh we speak the same," This was a discovery and recognition of their worth, their power, as they're going along: "Let's listen to that guy, he seems to know what he's doing. Let's go that way guys," and suddenly what appears initially as acts of spontaneity begin to acquire rhythm. The rhythm is people basically recognizing regularities: "Oh if I throw that, it hits,

*okay, we'll do it again." Slowly things begin to take shape.
I don't think anyone, even now, who took part in any of those
things would say they regretted it. Do they now think it was
something good to do? Not necessarily. I don't know anyone
who said, "I'm really sorry that we went on the street and
burnt down the building," well I haven't met one.*

JL: Let's jump to the present. At this moment, we don't
seem to have resolved the issues from the 1980s, but
how are they different? I'm of course thinking about Brexit
and the election of Trump, a general fear of globalization.
What have we gained over the years, and what have we
maybe also lost? Or, what have we not yet achieved?

*JA: If you make it more local, it helps to understand a little
bit more. If you take London as a kind of microcosm of the
neoliberal universe at the moment. Is it the case that to
live in London as a person of color now feels less frightening,
less oppressive than it was 30 years ago? Absolutely.
Because we are sitting now in a regenerated Dalston.
However, a mile and a half down the road, 25 years ago,
we would be demonstrating, because an area called
Shoreditch or Hoxton had members of the Far Right, the
National Front, selling neo-Nazi newspapers. If they saw an
Asian individual, he would be in trouble. So yes, for sure,
things have changed quite radically. Has that then gotten rid
of the question of the racial and how it impinges on life here?
I don't think so. This is the weird thing, it doesn't feel as
if it's a constant, it feels to me as if the ways in which
difference becomes a point of antagonism here changes
pending on other changes. Clearly one of the things that
triggered Brexit, and the desire for it, was this feeling that
somehow your average xenophobe couldn't control their
borders anymore. They were quite happy for all the other
features of the neoliberal order to be in place but didn't*

quite want it to extend to people. The conversation here at the moment has become one where they say, why can't the Europeans just grow up, accept, give us a deal, why do they need to keep fussing? Really, when you hear people who want to leave speak about Brexit, that's what they say. What they really mean is, we want a deal that allows us to have the French wine, the Mexican avocado, and the Kenyan beans, we just don't want the people. So, yes, Brexit with free trade but no free movement.

There's this weird way in which even though that is being said allegedly about Romanians or Poles, you feel as a person of color that it's about you. You feel as if something about your life has been a waste of time. I've been here over 50 years, and it feels like nothing I embodied, nothing about my "implications" offered any assuring example to calm people's fears, to accept that difference was not a bad thing. Certainly, in this place that's what it feels like, but it's clear that this is now responding to a much larger global picture, in which people have a very complex relation to the globalized present. They know that it means open borders, they know that it means free trade, they know that it means the movement of goods and so on, and they'd like to cherry-pick a little bit more. They'd like some of it and not the rest of it. But the package is not going to work. I'm not sure a package presented in those terms works.

JL: To quote Stuart Hall from The Unfinished Conversation, when he says "Identity is an endless ever unfinished conversation," where would you say that we are with the conversation, the debate with identity today?

JA: I think today certainly flux would be one, but also multiplicity. You feel as if different conversations are happening simultaneously around questions of identity. Which are both good but also bewildering, for sure. For instance, when I was in my teens, it felt as if all conversations about race were all about me, whether I was troubled or not. That seemed to be the only conversation. Now that language of migration and the discussion around migration is not taking place with the same intensity but it's now taking place alongside ones on reproductive rights, same-sex marriage, etc. There's a whole range of unfinished conversations that are in the process of becoming, or continuing, if you will. Suddenly you don't feel quite alone, but you also feel as if things are slightly more fractured at the same time and that the possibility of resolution is a slightly more complicated question now than it was before. Before, it was not that I by any means thought that everybody else was free except me, but you were made to feel as if you were the thing that stood in the way of everything good happening. That it was your fault, as migrants. If only you weren't here, this place would be great. And it turned out that actually there were a few more things not quite right with this place and most of them have very little to do with you. And that was a good thing to learn.

JL: I'm going to take you to 1995. The year that you made The Last Angel of History. Could you maybe talk about the film, and why you made it? How did it come about?

JA: The Last Angel of History is so strange because it's the one project that we did that when we finished it, I thought, okay, we don't have to return to this [laughing]. We're done. Because it seemed like one of those pieces you make to initiate a conversation, once that conversation is in motion you can kind of go back. Or move on. And the conversation really was threefold. One, we wanted to raise this specter of the unpopular as a defining black cultural norm, because the flipside was so in your face, black pop culture. Then there was the need to find a way of engaging the conversation

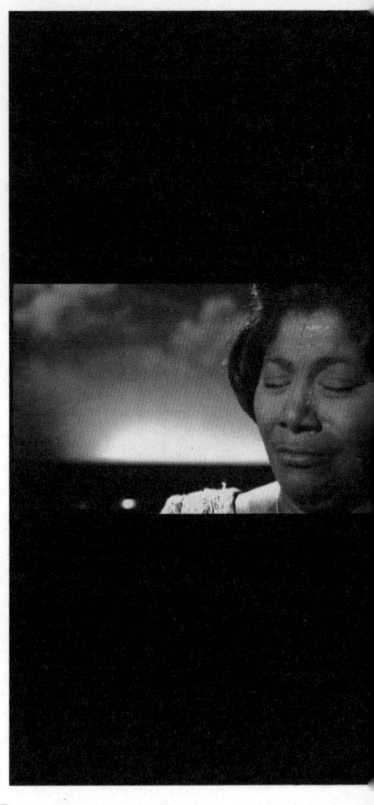

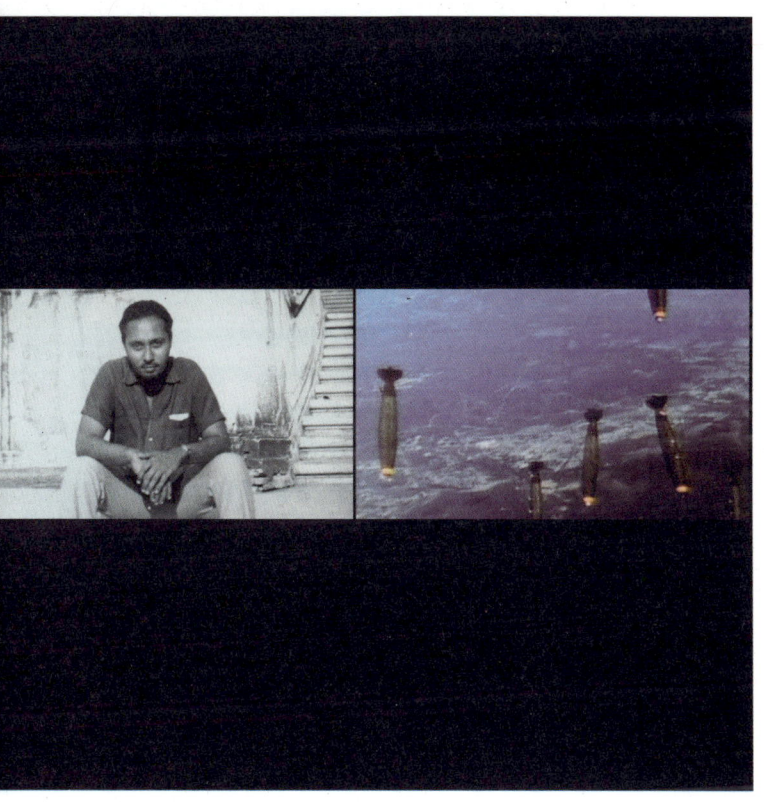

The Unfinished Conversation (2012) is the intimate and engaging portrait of Stuart Hall (1932–2014), the Jamaican-born pubic intellectual and cofounder of the *New Left Review*, whose work in cultural studies profoundly influenced the political and academic landscape. Weaving between the musical archaeology of Miles Davis and the political narratives of the twentieth century, the work carefully constructs archival sequences of rare, forgotten and historical material. The film pioneers a new archival and sonic approach to forgotten histories, forgotten ideas, and the untold stories of the politics of change.

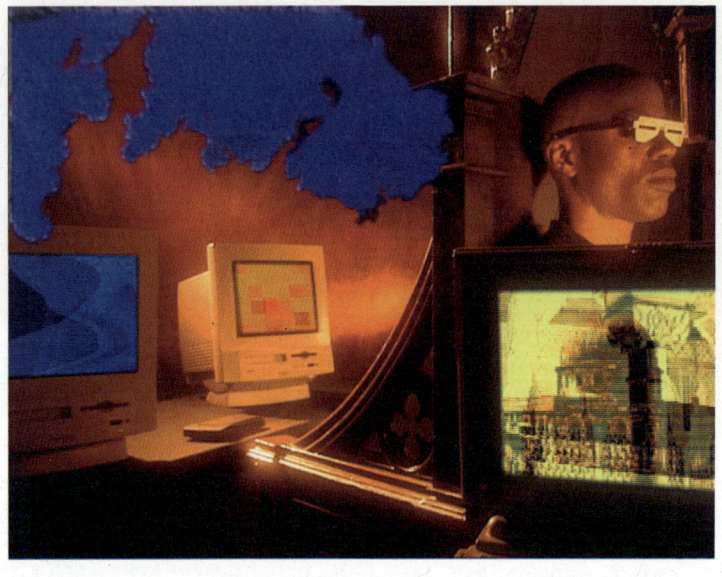

The Last Angel of History (1996) is a sci-fi documentary about Africa, history, and memory. Legend has it that in the 1930s itinerant bluesman Robert Johnson sold his soul to the devil in order to play the blues. What Johnson got in return for his soul was a black secret: technology that would produce the history of black music. Two hundred years into the future another itinerant figure, the Data Thief, sells his soul for the knowledge of his future. He has been told to go to the past (our present) and unearth black culture's speculations about the future.

The film explores the chromatic possibilities of digital video is embedded within a mythology of the future that creates connections between black unpopular culture, outer space, and the limits of the human condition.

on the technology in a way that brought people together. The one thing that The Last Angel of History has, that we've always tried to do, is to invoke the polyglot. If you said you were going to try to map out something called Afrofuturism, one of the possibilities this ambition seemed to license was a way of bringing together musicians, theorists, novelists, writers, and thinkers of all kinds together in order to just ponder this question in an open-ended way. Afrofuturism did seem like something on the horizons.

JL: Can you explain Afrofuturism in your own words?

JA: Afrofuturist musings were really about the idea that there might be a strand of black thought in the last century, which was interested in questions of science fiction, was interested in questions of black futures, interested in creating a kind of mythos of a black past in which one could disavow some things and take them back at the same time. So, you could say, yes, I am an African (British subject) a descendant of an enslaved African, but I also refuse to accept that, that's not just me, I am also descendent of the fugitive, of marronage. I am from Drexciya, I am a descendant of Dogon country from the Dogon in West Africa. In other words, Afrofuturism for me was always about black self-invention. A self-invention that involved the borrowings from speculative fiction, from science fiction, from music, to create this kind of hybrid form. That's what we thought it meant, and it's become a whole other thing since then, in a good way. But that's where we started from. If you told me then that there would be a Black Panther film that would gross two billion, no, I would not have believed that. Am I glad it's happened in that way? Yes, of course.

JL: If we could stay just in 1995, it seems like a time where there almost seems to be some kind of optimism.

Am I right? An optimism through both music and technology?

JA: Yes. This was the period of Samuel Delany, Donna Haraway, and Octavia Butler. Some of us were encountering these writings for the first time. On the eve of the cybernetic future about to come. The digital remained then just this kind of holy grail, not just something owned by Apple and Amazon. It seemed like it offered a possibility of some kind of techno-egalitarian future. So yes, you're right, there was definitely more optimism, and definitely more of a sense of a kind of impending egalitarian dawn, in which some of the older questions of ownership, wealth, and property and class were going to be resolved. They were going to be resolved by the right combination of populace, technology, and application, you sort of felt that. Then, of course, in a way that's what's happened. There's been this kind of massive democratization of the space of consumption, taste, but also by just massively exploding the numbers of us who are consumers. Not necessarily citizens, but consumers. Of course, the big corporations would argue, that actually if they improve your position as a consumer, then they do so for you as a citizen. That may well be true, but that's not the experience that I have. I don't get the sense that people are more powerful, that they control their lives more now than they did in the '90s. But do they have more access to other spaces in which they might exercise their being, yes, that feels true to me.

It feels as if, and this is a good thing, there were these huge conglomerates called countries and continents in which you could ascribe behavior patterns and ways of being and consuming trends to these vast spaces. And lo and behold, you introduce, you enter the digital world and these highly stratified spaces start to come apart at the seams and in ways that are both liberating and bewildering. You just have to go to a coffee shop in America to get a sense of the incredible diversity of taste [laughing], because, of course, 25 years ago, it was "A cup of coffee and some milk, please." That sort of Starbucks experience appears to be a defining feature of every avenue of life, and I think that's a good thing. That discovery of difference and the reach of that difference is a good thing.

People have things that they want to do, they have interests and hobbies, passions, loves, and desires that just couldn't be met because they were treated as whole things. Of course, somebody would make a huge ton of money from it, but it's happening all the same. If you are a young black man in London who overwhelmingly white taxi drivers wouldn't stop for in the center of town, now you don't have to deal with that, you just call an Uber and an Uber will come. At the same time, it also does feel as if there are some really dark features about the present. It's a space in which anonymity is granted to certain very cruel things and figures have been just unleashed, almost like in Yeats's poem "The Second Coming" where "mere anarchy is loosed upon the world." The fact that you have something called the "dark web" tells you everything you need to know: that there are basically other avenues of life which have been brought into being by this technology that are not "user-friendly."

CONVERSATIONS ACROSS TIME

JL: I want to talk about beauty and horror in your works. I don't find that you are judging in your films, but you are walking a fine line between the beauty and the horror of these things happening in our society. For instance, in The Unfinished Conversation, there's this sequence where you have mixed on three screens a famous hymn sung by black singer Mahalia Jackson. You have a sequence of an airplane dropping bombs, you have a child reading "The Tyger" by

William Blake, and then a clip of Stuart Hall talking about what that poem means to him, and then switching to footage of a child being born. And it's such a horrible but also such a beautiful sequence happening at the same time. So, I would like to know, what beauty means to you, and how do you work with it?

JA: When you say that you're interested in the archival, especially in the televisual form, it arrives at your doorstep in manifold ways. So, for instance I order material from '67 and I say to the archive give me everything you've got in this new strand on '67. And when it arrives, yes, of course, there's births but there's deaths and there's wars. Normally you would say, well I'm not interested in that, but if you don't have a particular agenda, if you're not trying to tell the story of a crime or if what you are trying to do is not really to "tell a story" at all. If, in fact, you're merely trying to gather moments from the past, especially a very specific year, then you are forced at some point to work out what would happen if you put these different moments that are coming to you as separate moments, if you tried to get them to coexist. It doesn't have to be necessarily birth and death, the birth and death one is a particularly beautiful one for me, because all of it could be emanating from the same village. Let's say that Mahalia Jackson is singing "Silent Night" on December 22, 1967. She's singing at the Hammersmith Odeon in West London. Now, just a mile away, at Charing Cross hospital a woman is also giving birth at exactly the same time and at that point in Mai Lai in Vietnam, in 1967, a soldier is dying. So, on one level, all I am doing is just alluding to the coexistence of these things. That soldier may well have come from Hammersmith born in that same hospital for all we know. So, things can germinate from the same space even though they get to exist in different times. Things can also arrive in different times and coexist in the same space. Both are

*confounding but also mesmerizing and occasionally beautiful
and occasionally disturbing.*

JL: Let me finish with a question on the conversation as
a leitmotif. We could maybe call your way of working as
conversations across time. You make people talk to each
other across time. For instance, when you are not able to
find material on Buddy Bolden, you make him have a
conversation with W. E. B. Du Bois or Booker T. Washington
in Precarity, people who lived at the same time. Or in
The Unfinished Conversation you make Stuart Hall and
Miles Davis have a conversation. Could we talk about what
conversations are? And what they do?

*JA: I never thought about that. Sometimes putting two
people together or two motifs together is merely a way of
pointing to those differences and similarities. So, Miles Davis
is a musician, Stuart Hall is a thinker, there's supposed to
be no logical connection to them, but actually when you
approach both of them, you see that there are all kinds of
similarities. One of the main ones is that they both seem
to have this real respect for the present, for conjunctures
and a need to situate their thinking or their practice and
performance at the forefront of those. To be in their moment,
as it were. So that was easy.*

*What's more difficult is to keep reminding yourself that
finding these unions is a way to perceive. I don't know why
that feels like an important need, but it does. Part of it is
simply the formal need for a counterpoint, to use a musical
analogy, a sort of response to a call from somewhere else.
In that sense you're right, it is a leitmotif in the work.*

*I've worked pretty much in communal spaces all my
life. I've worked in collectives all my life. I've partly liked
working with time-based work in that time too, because it's
so collaborative, communal, and collective. So clearly, it's*

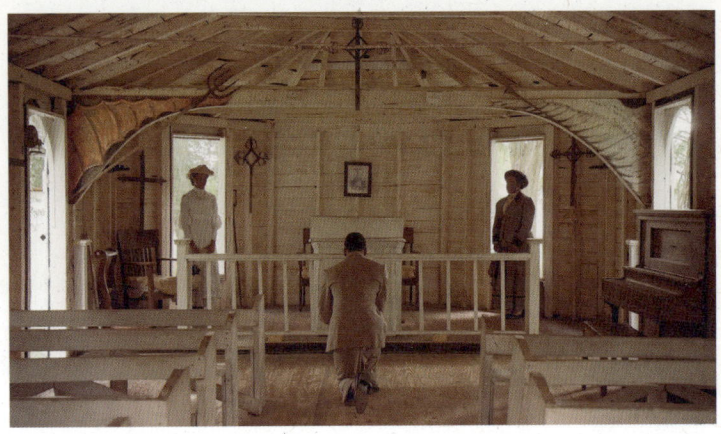

Precarity (2017) charts the dark tragedy of Charles Joseph "Buddy" Bolden the undisputed king of New Orleans music scene in the early 1900s. Institutionalized in his early thirties and never seen in public again, *Precarity* is an exploration of the diasporic condition, the legacy of creativity, displacement, and dispossession. Bolden's booming cornet and itinerant musical style is apocryphally famed as creating the sound of modern jazz. With no surviving recordings of Bolden's music, only myth and legend remain. As much a ghost story as it is a portrait of a historical figure, *Precarity* weaves together fragmented histories and archival remnants to connect the experience of those suffering at the violent ends of history and state power.

more than just an aesthetic. There's also a kind of emotional
want for collaboration and to therefore also try to see it
manifest in how the work operates. Now, if you were to
push me on that, I think the notion of the commonwealth
is quite important. It feels like I would have failed if I had
passed through and not had a conversation with people.
It would feel a failure. For histories, characters, moments
that have disappeared, these are important ways in which
one can retrieve things. Almost—to use a mountaineering
analogy—to be strapped to another being, that's for me
quite a beautiful thing to watch and see.

   You see the effort that each is having to make for
themselves, each component is having to make to stay in the
game. Crucially, there is also the question of the game in the
sense, and the ideal, that there might be something to play
for, enough people, enough beings and things, buy into the
rules of the game. This is really important to me, because
that seems to me to be the informal contract for spectatorship
in general.

   It is important for people who come to see works to, at
the very least, accept the premise that this is a multiscreen
piece, for instance, that they are going to be presented with
multiple perspectives, simultaneously, not necessarily all the
time, but quite a lot of the time, and that you accept that this
is a legitimate mode of exposition.

John Akomfrah is an artist and filmmaker, who was a founding member of the influential Black Audio Film Collective, which started in London in 1982. Since 1998 he has worked together with other founding members Lina Gopaul and David Lawson in the production collective Smoking Dogs Films. Together, they have produced large works such as Handsworth Songs *(1986)*, The Unfinished Conversation *(2012)*, Peripeteia *(2012)*, Mnemosyne *(2010)*, Vertigo Sea *(2015)*, and Purple *(2017)*, which have been shown at important venues such as the Imperial War Museum in London, New Museum in New York, Bildmuseet in Umeå, the 56th Venice Biennale, Sharjah Biennial 11, and Taipei Biennial in 2012.

Johanne Løgstrup is a curator and a PhD student in the Department of Aesthetics and Culture, Aarhus University, Denmark, where she is part of the research project The Contemporary Condition. Previously she cofounded the organization publik, ran the project space bureau public from 2012 to 2014 together with curator Katarina Stenbeck, and has worked as a curator at Nikolaj Kunsthal in Copenhagen. Among other exhibitions she curated "Museet er lukket" (The Museum Is Closed) at Nikolaj Kunsthal (2015), and the exhibition "Vertigo Sea" by John Akomfrah with the additional discursive program "Unfinished Histories," also at Nikolaj Kunsthal (2016).

PEN = 0,2,1,0, WEIGHT = 70, SLANT = 0, SUPERNESS = 0.65
PEN = 0,3,2,30, WEIGHT = 60, SLANT = .3, SUPERNESS = 0.7
PEN = 0,3,2,30, WEIGHT = 60, SLANT = -.3, SUPERNESS = 0.7

The typeface used to set this series is called Meta-the-difference-between-the-two-Font (MTDBT2F), designed by Dexter Sinister in 2010 after MetaFont, a digital typography system originally programmed by computer scientist Donald Kunth in 1979.

Unlike more common digital outline fonts formats such as TrueType or Postscript, a MetaFont is constructed of strokes drawn with set-width pens. Instead of describing each of the individual shapes that make up a family of related characters, a MetaFont file describes only the basic pen path or *skeleton* letter. Perhaps better imagined as the ghost that comes in advance of a particular letterform, a MetaFont character is defined only by a set of equations. It is then possible to tweak various parameters such as weight, slant, and superness (more or less bold, italic, and a form of chutzpah) in order to generate endless variations on the same bare bones.

Meta-the-difference-between-the-two-Font is essentially the same as MetaFont, abiding the obvious fact that it swallows its predecessor. Although the result may look the same, it clearly can't be, because in addition to the software, the new version embeds its own backstory. In this sense, MTDBT2F is not only a tool to generate countless PostScript fonts, but *at least equally* a tool to think about and around MetaFont. Mathematician Douglas Hofstadter once noted that one of the best things MetaFont might do is inspire readers to chase after the intelligence of an alphabet, and "yield new insights into the elusive "spirits" that flit about so tantalizingly behind those lovely shapes we call "letters.'"

For instance, each volume in The Contemporary Condition is set in a new MTDBT2F (or in this case three MTDBT2Fs), generated at the time of publication, which is to say *now.*

Dexter Sinister, 12/08/20, 13:10 AM